Celtic
VECTOR MOTIFS

By Alan Weller.
Designed by Joel Waldrep.

Celtic Vector Motifs is a new work, first published by Dover Publications, Inc., in 2010.

The CD-ROM file names correspond to the images in the book. All of the artwork stored on the CD-ROM can be imported directly into a wide range of design and word-processing programs on either Windows or Macintosh platforms. In order to take full advantage of the unique capabilities of the vector format images you will need a vector-editing program such as Adobe Illustrator or CorelDRAW. As a bonus, we have included the freeware vector editor Inkscape on this CD. For more information, see the Read Me! file in the Inkscape folder on the CD. For the most up-to-date information about using the image files on this CD, please visit www.doverpublications.com/991091.

ISBN 10: 0-486-99109-1
ISBN 13: 978-0-486-99109-2

Manufactured in the United States by Courier Corporation
99109101
www.doverpublications.com

001

002

003

004

005

006

007

1

008

009

010

011

012

013

014

015

016

017

018

019

020

021

3

023

022

024

025

026

027

028

4

029

030

031

032

033

034

035

036

037

038

039

040

041

042

043

044

045

046

047

048

049

050

051

8

052

053

054

055

056

057

9

058

059

060

061

062

063

10

064

065

066

067

068

069

070

071

072

073

074

075

076

077

078

079

080

081

082

083

084

085

14

086

087

088

089

090

091

092

093

094

095

096

097

098

099

100

101

102

103

104

105

106

107

108

109

110

111

112

113

114

115

116

117

118

119

120

121

122

123

124

125

126

127

128

129

130

131

132

133

134

135

136

137

138

140

139

141

142

143

144

145

146

147

148

149

150

151

152

153

154

24

155

156

157

159

160

158

161

162

163

164

165

166

167

168

169

170

171

172

173

174

175

27

176

177

178

179

180

181

182

183

184

185

186

187

29

188

189

190

191

192

193

194

195

196

197

198

199

200

201

202

symbol for st. luke
203

204

205

206

207

208

209

210

211

symbol for st. mark

212

213

214

215

216

217

218

219

220

221

222

223

224

225

226

227

228

229

35

230

231

232

233

234

235

symbol for St. John
238

236

237

239

240

241

242

243

37

244

245

246

247

248

249

250

251

252

253

254

255

256

257

39

258

259

symbol for st. matthew

260

261

262

263

264

265

266

267

268 269 270

41

271

272

273

274

275

276

277

278

279

280

281

282

283

284

285

286

287

288

289

290

291

292

293

294

295

296

297

298

299

300

302

301

303

304

305

306

307

308

309